WE SHALL OVERCOME

THE CIVIL RIGHTS ACT
OF 1964

A PRIMARY SOURCE EXPLORATION OF THE LANDMARK LEGISLATION

by Heather E. Schwartz

Consultant:
Bruce Allen Murphy, PhD
Fred Morgan Kirby Professor of Civil Rights
Lafayette College
Easton, Pennsylvania

CAPSTONE PRESS
a capstone imprint

Fact Finders Books are published by Capstone Press,
1710 Roe Crest Drive, North Mankato, Minnesota 56003
www.capstonepub.com

Library of Congress Cataloging-in-Publication Data
Schwartz, Heather E., author.
The Civil Rights Act of 1964 : a primary source exploration of the landmark legislation / by Heather E. Schwartz.
pages cm. — (Fact finders. We shall overcome.)
Includes bibliographical references and index.
Summary: "Uses primary sources to explore the passage of the Civil Rights Act of 1964"— Provided by publisher.
ISBN 978-1-4914-0224-5 (library binding) — ISBN 978-1-4914-0233-7 (pbk.) — ISBN 978-1-4914-0229-0 (ebook pdf)
1. United States. Civil Rights Act of 1964—Juvenile literature. 2. Civil rights—United States—History—20th century—
Juvenile literature. I. Title.
KF4750.S35 2015
342.7308'5—dc23   2014009588

Editorial Credits
Jennifer Besel, editor; Cynthia Akiyoshi, designer; Wanda Winch, media researcher;
    Charmaine Whitman, production specialist

Photo Credits
AP Images, 29, Richard Drew, 19 (bottom); Corbis: Bettmann, 16, 19 (top), Hulton-Deutsch Collection, 17; Courtesy
of Arkansas Democrat-Gazette, cover (background), 22; Getty Images Inc: CBS Photo Archive, 26, Paris Match/
Paul Slade, 20, Popperfoto/Rolls Press, 27; John F. Kennedy Campaign Brochure, America Votes, 1960, United States
Political Campaign Materials Collection, David M. Rubenstein Rare Book & Manuscript Library, Duke University,
13 (all); The John F. Kennedy Presidential Library and Museum, 15; Library of Congress: Prints and Photographs
Division, 7, 11, 14; Lyndon Baines Johnson Library: Cecil Stoughton, cover, 5, Yoichi Okamoto, 23, 25; McCain Library
and Archives, The University of Southern Mississippi, 9 (b); National Archives and Records Administration, 21,
Records of the National Park Service, 9 (t); Newscom: KRT, 10; Shutterstock: Olga k, paper background, Picsfive,
paper pieces

Printed in the United States of America in Stevens Point, Wisconsin.
032014   008092WZF14

TABLE OF CONTENTS

A NOTE ABOUT PRIMARY SOURCES

Primary sources are newspaper articles, photographs, speeches, or other documents that were created during an event. They are great ways to see how people spoke and felt during that time. You'll find primary sources from the time of the debate and passage of the Civil Rights Act of 1964 throughout this book. Within the text, these primary sources are colored blue and set in italic type.

Chapter One
SIGNED INTO LAW

It was July 2, 1964. U.S. President Lyndon B. Johnson sat at a table in the White House's East Room. With a pen in hand, he was ready to sign the paperwork before him.

Behind him politicians and civil rights leaders stood ready as witnesses. In front of him, TV cameras captured the historic moment.

Before signing, Johnson explained what his signature on the paperwork would mean. *"We believe that all men are created equal. Yet many are denied equal treatment ... The reasons are deeply imbedded in history and tradition and the nature of man. We can understand ... how this all happened. But it cannot continue. Our Constitution, the foundation of our Republic, forbids it. The principles of our freedom forbid it. **Morality** forbids it. And the law I will sign tonight forbids it."*

morality—beliefs about what is right or wrong

4

► Photographer Cecil Stoughton captured President Lyndon Johnson signing the Civil Rights Act as lawmakers and civil rights leaders looked on.

On that day the Civil Rights Act became law. The law would protect the rights of all Americans—no matter what the color of their skin. But passing a law protecting civil rights was no easy matter. It required a long, hard struggle.

Chapter Two
SOUTHERN SEGREGATION

Before the Civil Rights Act of 1964, laws in the southern United States **segregated** blacks and whites. African-Americans were forced to use separate public spaces, including parks, pools, bathrooms, schools, and hotels. The public facilities for black people weren't as good as those for whites. Sometimes they didn't exist at all. For example, some bus stations had just one waiting room marked "Whites Only." In that case black passengers had to wait outside.

Emily Tynes of the American Civil Liberties Union grew up in the segregated south. She remembers running an errand for her mother as a child. *"I boarded the segregated city bus and took the first available seat, which happened to be in the front. The bus driver pointed to the rear and told me to go sit there. That was the moment I realized my mother did not sit on the back of the bus because she preferred to, but because she had no choice."*

segregate—to keep people of different races apart in schools and other public places

COLORED
WAITING ROOM

PRIVATE PROPERTY
NO PARKING
Driving through or Turning Around

▶ Bus stations throughout the South had clearly divided spaces for passengers, like this station in Durham, North Carolina.

CAROLINA COACH COMPANY

A Mass Movement

African-Americans and many whites protested the **discrimination**. By the 1950s black leaders such as the Rev. Dr. Martin Luther King Jr. were organizing mass nonviolent protests. Thousands of people joined the cause, marching with banners and singing freedom songs. These protests became known as the civil rights movement.

Some white southerners were prepared to fight to make sure segregation stayed in place. In 1961 black and white activists called Freedom Riders disobeyed segregation laws on buses. Mobs greeted the riders at bus stations with clubs and fists. The media reported on an attack in Alabama. *"There were from 300 to 1,000 whites in the area of the bus depot. Before police finally broke up the crowd with tear gas, [the mob] beat and injured at least 20 persons of both races ..."*

Even when they were attacked, however, protesters did not fight back. Civil rights activist Gordon Carey said, *"[The activists] believed that the best way to approach a problem was through ... directly confronting it but not responding in any way with any violence."*

discrimination—treating people unfairly because of their race, country of birth, or gender

Even children joined the civil rights movement. On October 25, 1959, students marched in Washington, D.C., for integrated schools.

Meeting Nonviolence with Violence

Activists in the civil rights movement worked toward desegregation through nonviolent protests. But many white people responded to the protests with violence. The Ku Klux Klan (KKK) is an organization whose members believe white people are superior to black people. The KKK regularly harassed, attacked, and even murdered people who worked to end segregation. *"The eyes of the KKK are watching you,"* a 1957 flyer read. *"Please take warning."*

The First Civil Rights Act

In 1956 U.S. Attorney General Herbert Brownell Jr. felt it was time for federal lawmakers to get involved. He proposed a civil rights bill to Congress that addressed voting rights and justice in the legal system. It would also give black students the right to attend the same schools as white students.

Many Southern politicians didn't like the bill. In fact Senator Strom Thurmond from South Carolina was so against it, he decided to use a **filibuster**. He spoke for 24 hours and 18 minutes to prevent Congress from voting. Near the end of his speech, Thurmond said, *"... I felt that this bill was of such importance ... that it was my duty to make sure that I had not failed to exert every effort again to emphasize the dangers of the bill."*

▶ Senator Strom Thurmond

FACT

During his filibuster Senator Thurmond read voting laws state by state and the Declaration of Independence. It still holds the record for longest filibuster in U.S. history.

Lawmakers battled back and forth on the bill. Eventually, they agreed on a compromise version. The law they passed was said to protect voting rights. But lawmakers did not set up ways to **enforce** the law. Roy Wilkins, executive secretary of the National Association for the Advancement of Colored People (NAACP), said it was only *"a small crumb from Congress."*

▶ Roy Wilkins

filibuster—an effort to prevent action by making a long speech

enforce—to make sure something happens

Chapter Three

A NEW PRESIDENT

The Civil Rights Act of 1957 did little to give African-Americans the same rights as whites. However, many hoped it was a first step toward more change. When Senator John F. Kennedy ran for president in 1960, he made it clear he supported the civil rights movement.

Kennedy publicly promised to desegregate public housing *"by a stroke of the presidential pen."* In a presidential debate against his opponent, Vice President Richard Nixon, Kennedy strongly stated his support for civil rights. *"I'm not satisfied until every American enjoys his full constitutional rights. If a Negro baby is born ... he has about one-half as much chance to get through high school as a white baby ... I think we can do better."*

Nixon responded to Kennedy's remarks. *"... Senator Kennedy has suggested in his speeches that we lack compassion for ... others that are unfortunate ... our disagreement is not about the goals for America but only about the means to reach those goals."*

Kennedy's words were what civil rights activists needed to hear. They supported him with their votes.

Human rights
Kennedy cares
Kennedy acts

A time for moral LEADERSHIP

"We seek to secure these rights"

1. The right of every American to work as he wants to work.

2. The right of every American to be educated.

3. The right of every American to receive just compensation for his labor, his crops, his goods.

4. The right of every American to live in a decent home in a neighborhood of his choice.

5. The right of every American to obtain security in sickness as well as health.

6. The right of every American to think, to vote, to speak, to read, to worship as he pleases.

7. The right of all people to be free from the terrors of war.

... *Senator Kennedy*
NAACP Rally, Los Angeles

WINNING TEAM

Senator Lyndon B. Johnson of Texas is the Democratic candidate for Vice President. As Senate Majority Leader he led the fight for the enactment of the Civil Rights Bills of 1957 and 1960. Senator Johnson has pledged to "campaign from one coast to the other on the platform of the Democratic party."

VOTE DEMOCRATIC

KENNEDY
FOR PRESIDENT
JOHNSON
FOR VICE PRESIDENT

KENNEDY
for PRESIDENT

[1960]

Senator Kennedy confers with African leader Tom Mboya

...segregation plans in *all* school districts by 1963.

5. An end to literacy tests and poll taxes.
6. A change of Senate rules to end filibustering.

...that the goals of the Democratic civil rights plank can only be achieved by strong moral leadership from the White House. "That leadership must be exercised until every American, of every color and faith, has achieved equal access to the voting booth, to the schoolroom, to jobs, to housing and to lunch counters."

SIT-IN DEMONSTRATORS

Senator Kennedy, for 14 years a fighter for civil rights, was one of the first national leaders to support peaceful sit-in demonstrations. "It is in the American tradition to stand up for one's rights — even if the new way to stand up for one's rights is to sit down."

AFRICAN AFFAIRS

Senator Kennedy is Chairman of the Senate Foreign Relations Subcommittee on Africa. He has focused Senate — and national — attention on the problems of Africa and other underdeveloped parts of the world. "The American dream of 1776 is now the African dream — together, Africa and America must dedicate themselves to fulfilling that dream for all mankind."

▶ When running for president, Kennedy made his stance on civil rights clear. This campaign brochure explained to voters what rights Kennedy hoped to secure for African-Americans.

Growing Frustration

Once Kennedy became president, however, he didn't push for civil rights changes as voters had hoped. Kennedy was busy with foreign affairs. He also felt that in order to keep the support of Southern politicians, he'd have to make changes slowly. African-Americans weren't happy when he stalled on signing an order to desegregate public housing. *"[M]onths went by without the stroke [of the presidential pen]. Negroes grew impatient, took to mailing him pens as sarcastic reminders,"* Time magazine reported in November 1962.

Meanwhile, the tension between blacks and whites in the South continued to boil. In Albany, Georgia, activists tried to desegregate the entire city by disobeying segregation laws. There were mass arrests and violence.

▶ Albany, Georgia, police chief Laurie Pritchett ordered officers to arrest large groups of activists to silence the civil rights movement in his city.

In December 1961 King sent a telegram to Kennedy, asking for support from the federal government. But Kennedy did not get the federal government involved.

▶ King's telegram said, *"We urge you issue at once by executive order a second emancipation proclamation to free all Negroes from second class citizenship ... We urge you further to ... release at once the hundreds of persons now in jail in Albany Georgia ..."*

Small Steps

Kennedy didn't take quick action as activists wanted. But in the early part of his presidency, he did do things to help the civil rights movement. In 1961 he pressured the Interstate Commerce Commission (ICC) to ban segregation on buses traveling between states. Then in 1962 he sent federal marshals to help a black student safely attend classes at the previously all-white University of Mississippi.

Chapter Four

CRISIS IN BIRMINGHAM

In 1963 the civil rights movement heated up in Birmingham, Alabama. It started when George C. Wallace was elected governor. That January, Wallace delivered a powerful speech. He vowed to defend the white South from integration. *"I say, segregation now, segregation tomorrow, and segregation forever."*

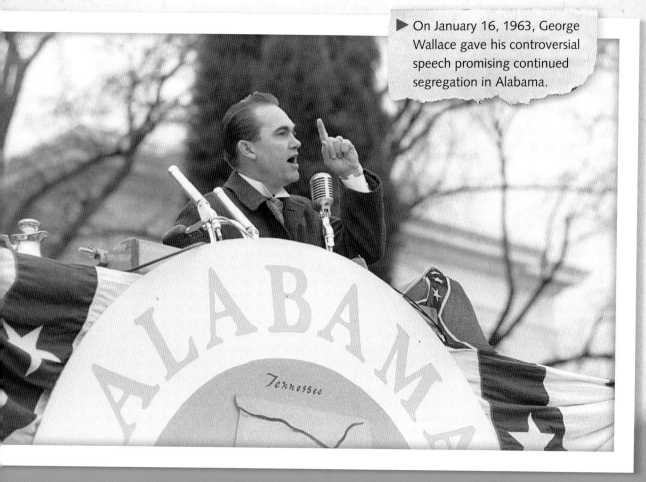

► On January 16, 1963, George Wallace gave his controversial speech promising continued segregation in Alabama.

Civil rights activists recognized the power of his words. *"Governor Wallace never pulled a trigger. He never fired a gun. But in his speech, he created the environment for others to pull the trigger, in the days, the weeks, and months to come,"* said civil rights activist John Lewis.

According to James L. Poe Jr., then-president of the Montgomery chapter of the NAACP, Wallace's words inspired violence almost immediately. *"We began to feel the sting of the speech. People night-riding and burning crosses,"* he said. *"The police beat down people and ran over them with horses, put tear gas on them."*

► Taken in 1965, this image captures the scene at a KKK meeting. KKK members often burned crosses in the yards of African-Americans as a way to scare them.

Throughout 1963 civil rights activists staged nonviolent marches, sit-ins, strikes, and demonstrations in Birmingham. King got involved and was jailed in April. He defended activists for breaking unjust laws in a letter published by the media. *"**Oppressed** people cannot remain oppressed forever. The yearning for freedom eventually **manifests** itself, and that is what has happened to the American Negro,"* he wrote.

In response to the protests, some officials in Birmingham turned violent. Firefighters used high-pressure water hoses to break up demonstrations. Police turned attack dogs on activists, allowing the dogs to lunge and bite.

The violence was reported around the world—and it was making the United States look terrible. As America's president, Kennedy had to take charge of the crisis.

FACT

Thousands of children joined the protests in Birmingham. Like adults, they were sprayed with fire hoses, attacked by police dogs, and arrested.

oppress—to be treated in a cruel, unjust, and hard way

manifest—to become shown or visible

► Firefighters sprayed activists with high-pressure hoses at close range in order to stop the protests.

► pages of King's handwritten "Letter from Birmingham Jail"

1 B

On that dramatic scene on Calvary's hill three men were crucified. We must never forget that all three were crucified for the same crime — the crime of extremism. Two were extremists for immorality, and thus fell below their environment. The other, Jesus Christ, was an extremist for love, truth, and goodness, and thereby rose above his environment.

2 B

I have been so greatly disappointed with the white Church and its leadership. Of course there are some notable exceptions. I am not unmindful of the fact that each of

2 B (Cont.)

I commend you, her Christian stand on the past Negroes in your worship segregated basis. I commend of this state for integrity several years ago. these notable exceptions I reiterate that I have been Church.

3 B

Christians entered a town the came disturbed and immediately for being "disturbers of the stors" But the Christians conviction that they were "a called to obey God rather than man. Small in number, they were big in commitment. They were too God-intoxicated

Chapter Five

A FEDERAL CALL TO ACTION

Soon Kennedy found the perfect opportunity to take charge. On June 11, 1963, two black students tried to register for classes at the University of Alabama. Governor Wallace stood in the doorway to prevent the students from entering. Wallace declared that forcing him to admit the students was a **violation** of Alabama's state rights. *"It is important that the people of this State and nation understand that this action is in violation of rights reserved to the State by the Constitution of the United States ..."*

The 1954 Supreme Court ruling in *Brown v. Board of Education* had made segregation in public schools illegal. To uphold the ruling, Kennedy sent in troops to force Wallace to move.

▶ Wallace's refusal to move became known as "The Stand in the Schoolhouse Door."

violation—an action that breaks a rule or a law

That same day Kennedy announced his plans for a Civil Rights Act that would fully protect black Americans' rights.

TCS - 2nd Draft
6/11/63

Good evening, my fellow Americans:

This afternoon, following a series of threats and defiant statements, the presence of Alabama National Guardsmen was required on the University of Alabama campus to carry out the final and unequivocal order of the United State District Court for the Northern District of Alabama. That order called for the admission of two clearly-qualified young Alabama residents who happened to have been born Negro.

I hope that every American, regardless of where he lives, will stop and examine his conscience about these and related events. This nation was founded by men of many nations and backgrounds. It was founded on the principle that all men are created equal -- and that the rights of every man are diminished when the rights of one are threatened. Today we are committed to a world-wide struggle to protect and promote the rights of all who wish to be free. And when Americans are sent to Vietnam or West

nd mine, we do not ask for whites only.

erefore, for American students of any

institution they select without having

be possible for American consumers

n places of public accommodation --

and retail stores -- without having

► The first page of Kennedy's speech announcing his plans for a Civil Rights bill talked about the events at the University of Alabama. Later in the speech he said, *"I am, therefore, asking the Congress to enact legislation giving all Americans the right to be served in facilities which are open to the public ... I am also asking Congress to authorize the Federal Government to participate more fully in lawsuits designed to end segregation in public education ..."*

Devastating News

With Kennedy's strong support and plans for new laws, civil rights activists were hopeful. But on November 22, 1963, that hope was crushed. Kennedy was **assassinated**. His death was a shocking blow to the country.

assassinate—to murder a person who is well known or important

▶ In December 1963 President Johnson (right) met with King in the Oval Office to talk about civil rights.

Vice President Lyndon B. Johnson took the presidential oath. No one knew what would happen to Kennedy's Civil Rights Act. Johnson's political history showed he often didn't support the civil rights movement.

But Johnson surprised many. When he took office, he spoke of Kennedy's dreams for the country. And he said he planned to support those dreams. *"... above all, the dream of equal rights for all Americans, whatever their race or color—these and other American dreams have been vitalized by [Kennedy's] drive and by his dedication. And now the ideas and the ideals which he so nobly represented must and will be translated into effective action."*

Debates

Johnson worked hard to get the Civil Rights Act passed. He used his friendships with senators to get enough votes to pass the bill. He also had a powerful personality. He wasn't afraid to charm and even threaten those he needed on his side. His assistant remembers Johnson's meeting with Georgia Senator Richard Russell, who opposed the bill. *"[President Johnson] said: 'Dick, you've got to get out of my way. I'm going to run over you ... don't stand in my way.'"*

On the Senate floor, many lawmakers spoke against the law. They spoke for 57 days straight, trying to stop it. Senator Thurmond declared that passing the act would *"mark one of the darkest days in history."*

Finally Minority Leader Everett Dirksen spoke in support of the bill. *"The time has come for equality of opportunity in sharing in government, in education, and in employment. It will not be stayed or denied. It is here!"*

When the Senate voted, the bill passed with just four votes more than were required. It only needed the House of Representatives' final approval and the president's signature to become law.

▶ Johnson used a tactic of going nose to nose with others to persuade them to vote a certain way. Photographer Yoichi Okamoto caught Johnson (left) using this technique on Senator Richard Russell on December 7, 1963.

A Historic Day

On July 2, 1964, just two days before the nation would celebrate its independence, Johnson signed the Civil Rights Act. He said of the law, *"Its purpose is not to divide but to end divisions—divisions which have lasted all too long."* The act gave independence to an entire race of people. The law banned segregation in stores, restaurants, schools, and libraries. It also banned discrimination. Employers could no longer refuse to hire people based on their color, race, religion, or gender.

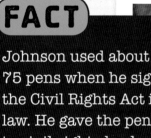

FACT

Johnson used about 75 pens when he signed the Civil Rights Act into law. He gave the pens to civil rights leaders and Congress members who worked to get the law passed.

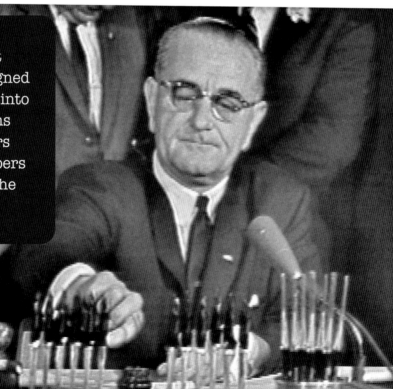

Civil rights leaders were pleased. *"This was the way to really save the nation. And [Johnson] knew it was not politically expedient, but I think he really knew it was right,"* recalled Andrew Young, a civil rights leader.

But the law did not immediately change life in the South. Many whites still disagreed with the Civil Rights Act. To avoid integration, many public places closed. In South Boston, Virginia, the newspaper reported such an event on July 23. *"Two Negro girls showed up at the white pool ... and pool lifeguards, acting on orders, immediately began draining the pool and later locked the gates."*

▶ In St. Augustine, Florida, activists tried to desegregate a motel pool. The manager poured liquid from containers marked "muriatic acid" into the water to force the swimmers to leave.

A Lasting Effect

In a June 1963 speech, Kennedy acknowledged that no law would be enough to guarantee civil rights. *"[Legislation] … cannot solve this problem alone. It must be solved in the homes of every American in every community across our country … My fellow Americans, this is a problem which faces us all—in every city of the North as well as the South."*

Segregation and discrimination still exist in the United States today. But the Civil Rights Act has made a difference. The law is a protection. When people's civil rights are violated, they can use the legal system to fight injustice.

Voting Rights Act

The Civil Rights Act did not address voting rights. But it did pave the way for a law that did. The Voting Rights Act passed in 1965. This law banned discrimination in voting. The Voting Rights Act made sure that everyone could vote for government leaders.

► In March 1964 a crowd of about 1,500 people marched in Tallahassee, Florida, to support the Civil Rights Act. The people in that crowd, and many others, believed the Civil Rights Act would be a major step toward equality for all people.

The Civil Rights Act of 1964 made major strides in the fight against segregation and discrimination. It helped minorities get hired for good jobs. In addition, it continues to make discrimination against other groups, such as women and other minorities, illegal. As Johnson said when he signed it, *"[the law's] purpose is to promote a more abiding commitment to freedom, a more constant pursuit of justice, and a deeper respect for human dignity."*

Selected Bibliography

"The First Kennedy-Nixon Presidential Debate." September 26, 1960. Online by the Commission on Presidential Debates. http://www.debates.org/index.php?page=september-26-1960-debate-transcript

"Freedom Riders: Watch the Full Film." American Experience, 2010. http://www.pbs.org/wgbh/americanexperience/freedomriders/watch

Johnson, Lyndon Baines. "Remarks upon Signing the Civil Rights Bill (July 2, 1964)." Online by Miller Center of Public Affairs at the University of Virginia. http://millercenter.org/president/speeches/detail/3525

Kennedy, John F. "Address on Civil Rights (June 11, 1963)." Online by Miller Center of Public Affairs at the University of Virginia. http://millercenter.org/president/speeches/detail/3375

King, Martin Luther, Jr. "December 13, 1961 Telegram" Online by the John F. Kennedy Presidential Library and Museum. http://www.jfklibrary.org/Asset-Viewer/9EKJbHBCsEaVSQuCdwdigA.aspx

King, Martin Luther, Jr. "Letter From Birmingham City Jail." Online by The King Center. http://www.thekingcenter.org/archive/document/letter-birmingham-city-jail-0

"Ku Klux Klan flyer circa November 1957." Online by the University of Southern Mississippi Digital Collections. http://digilib.usm.edu/cdm/ref/collection/manu/id/199

"President Johnson Signs Civil Rights Act of 1964." July 2, 1964. Online by C-Span. http://www.c-span.org/video/?300956-1/president-johnson-signs-civil-rights-act-1964

Radio Diaries. "'Segregation Forever': A Fiery Pledge Forgiven, But Not Forgotten." NPR. http://www.npr.org/2013/01/14/169080969/segregation-forever-a-fiery-pledge-forgiven-but-not-forgotten

Wallace, George C. "1963 Inaugural Speech" January 14, 1963. Online by the Alabama Department of Archives and History. http://www.youtube.com/watch?v=sMDWov-kGcQ

Glossary

assassinate (uh-SASS-uh-nate)—to murder a person who is well known or important

discrimination (dis-kri-muh-NAY-shuhn)—treating people unfairly because of their race, country of birth, or gender

enforce (in-FORS)—to make sure something happens

filibuster (FILL-uh-bus-ter)—an effort to prevent action by making a long speech

oppress (oh-PRESS)—to be treated in a cruel, unjust, and hard way

manifest (MAN-uh-fest)—to become shown or visible

morality (muh-RA-la-tee)—beliefs about what is right and wrong behavior

segregate (SEG-ruh-gate)—to keep people of different races apart in schools and other public places

violation (vye-oh-LAY-shun)—an action that breaks a rule or a law

Critical Thinking Using the Common Core

1. King's telegram to Kennedy on page 15 asked for "a second emancipation proclamation." What was King referring to? Use other resources to support your answer. (Integration of Knowledge and Ideas)

2. Compare the excerpt of Wallace's speech on page 16 with the quotation from Poe on page 17. What action words does each speaker use? How do those action words shape the tone of each message? (Craft and Structure)

Internet Sites

FactHound offers a safe, fun way to find Internet sites related to this book. All of the sites on FactHound have been researched by our staff.

Here's all you do:
Visit *www.facthound.com*
Type in this code: 9781491402245

Check out projects, games and lots more at
www.capstonekids.com

Index